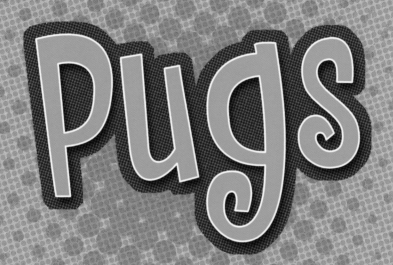

Pugs

Sarah Frank

Lerner Publications ◆ Minneapolis

Lerner Publications Company
A division of Lerner Publishing Group, Inc.
241 First Avenue North
Minneapolis, MN 55401 USA

For reading levels and more information, look up this title at www.lernerbooks.com.

Library of Congress Cataloging-in-Publication Data

Names: Frank, Sarah, author.
Title: Pugs / Sarah Frank.
Description: Minneapolis : Lerner Publications, [2019] | Series: Lightning bolt books. Who's a good dog? | Audience: Age 6–9. | Audience: Grade K to 3. | Includes bibliographical references and index.
Identifiers: LCCN 2018004399 | ISBN 9781541538597 (lb : alk. paper)
Subjects: LCSH: Pug—Juvenile literature.
Classification: LCC SF429.P9 F73 2019 | DDC 636.76—dc23

LC record available at https://lccn.loc.gov/2018004399

Manufactured in the United States of America
1-45042-35869-6/6/2018

Table of Contents

Hug a Pug

Do you want a dog that makes you smile? What about one that's playful and loving? If so, a pug may be for you!

Pugs are small but sturdy. They stand between 12 and 14 inches (30 and 36 cm) high. They weigh up to 18 pounds (8 kg).

This pug gets a gentle hug from its owner.

Pugs are tons of fun. They are friendly and outgoing. They also look great in dog clothes.

Pugs welcome visitors and play well with other pets. But they are happiest around their special humans. And those humans say pugs are the best!

Pugs make special family members.

Toy Dogs

Some dogs herd. Others hunt. Still others are extra cuddly. The American Kennel Club (AKC) groups similar dogs together. Pugs are in the toy group.

Most toy dogs love being extra close to their owners.

Dogs in the toy group are small. You may have stuffed animals bigger than they are! These dogs make wonderful pets.

Toy dogs come from many countries. Pugs come from China. These days, they are found all over the world.

Pugs are one of the most popular dog breeds.
Think you could love a pug?

Oh, that face!

Do You Want a Pug?

Pugs are sweet. Yet not everyone should get one. Decide with a parent whether a pug should join your family.

Brushing can cut down on shedding, but pugs still shed a lot.

Pugs shed. Pug owners find hair on their clothes. If you don't like dog hair, don't get a pug.

Pugs hate being alone. Do you have lots of after-school activities? Then a cat might make a better pet.

Bored dogs may chew on whatever they find.

Does your family want a watchdog? If so, pass on a pug. These friendly dogs may not even bark at a robber!

A pug is more likely to lick than to attack.

Pug Care

Let's say you've decided a pug is for you. Then you're going to need some supplies. Dogs need things like bowls, toys, and a leash.

A vet will take good care of your pug.

Take your pug to a vet right away. Vets check dogs for health problems. They also give pooches the shots they need.

Sometimes pugs need baths to stay clean.

Brush your pug a few times a week. This will remove loose hair. A pug's wrinkles need care too! Use a baby wipe to clean the folds in your dog's skin.

Your pug will be your new best friend. Play with it. Pet it. Give it lots of love.

What's better than loving a pug?

Doggone Good Tips!

- Give your pug a name both you and your pooch can be proud of. Here are some ideas: Snuggles, Gizmo, Pickle, Lola, Spike, Wrinkles, or Gordie.

- Keep your pug cool to keep it safe. Pugs can have a hard time breathing in hot weather. Make sure to let your pug out for just a few minutes at a time on very hot days.

- Pugs love food. But too much can make them sick. Use treats only when training your dog. And don't give your pug table scraps.

Why Pugs Are the Best

- Those tiny, curly tails! All puppy tails are cute, but pug puppies just may have the cutest tails of all.

- They have funny personalities. Many pug owners like to say that pugs are really clowns in dogs' bodies.

- The Duke and Duchess of Windsor loved them. This royal couple lived in France. In the 1940s, they had about eleven pugs.

Glossary

American Kennel Club (AKC): an organization that groups dogs by breed

breed: a particular type of dog. Dogs of the same breed have the same body shape and general features.

outgoing: friendly and at ease with different people and situations

shed: to lose hair

toy group: a group of different types of dogs that are all small in size

vet: a doctor who treats animals

Further Reading

American Kennel Club
http://www.akc.org

American Society for the Prevention of Cruelty to Animals
https://www.aspca.org

Barnes, Nico. *Pugs.* Minneapolis: Abdo Kids, 2015.

Fishman, Jon M. *Hero Therapy Dogs.* Minneapolis: Lerner Publications, 2017.

Gray, Susan H. *Pugs.* New York: AV2 by Weigl, 2017.

Index

Photo Acknowledgments

Image credits: Ezzolo/Shutterstock.com, pp. 2, 4, 8, 23; Serhiy Kobyakov/Shutterstock.com, p. 5; Martin Carlsson/Shutterstock.com, p. 6; India Picture/Shutterstock.com, p. 7; Annette Shaff/Shutterstock.com, p. 9; John Arsenault/The Image Bank/Getty Images, p. 10; Utekhina Anna/Shutterstock.com, p. 11; Nataliya Kuznetsova/Shutterstock.com, p. 12; Ariane Lohmar/Getty Images, p. 13; Aseph/Shutterstock.com, p. 14; Africa Studio/Shutterstock.com, p. 15; Bulltus_casso/Shutterstock.com, p. 16; Ariel Skelley/The Image Bank/Getty Images, p. 17; Sinseeho/Shutterstock.com, p. 18; XiXinXing/iStock/Getty Images, p. 19; studio22comua/iStock/Getty Images, p. 21.
Cover: GlobalP/iStock/Getty Images.

Main body text set in Billy Infant regular 28/36. Typeface provided by SparkType.